WITHDRAWN

2008
COMMEMORATIVE
STAMP
YEARBOOK

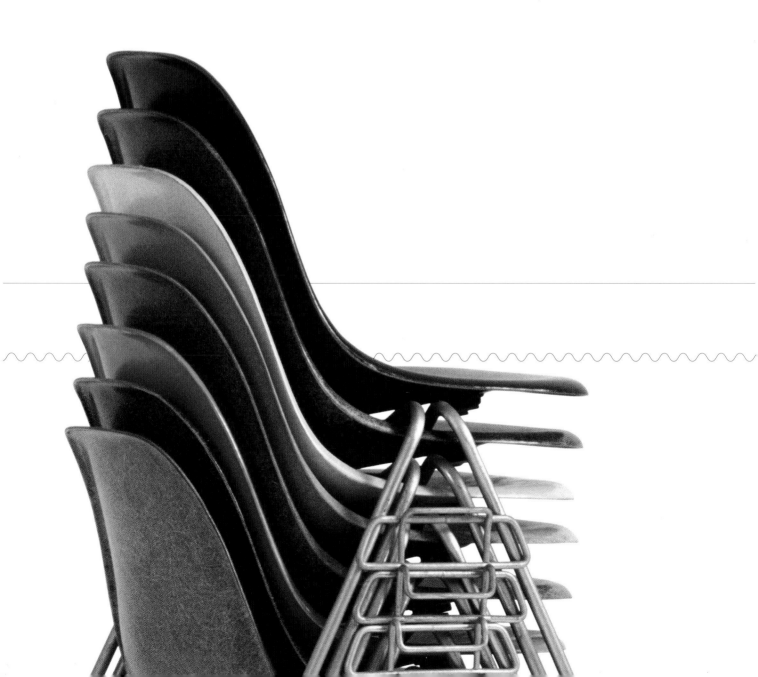

2008
COMMEMORATIVE
STAMP YEARBOOK

UNITED STATES
POSTAL SERVICE ®
www.usps.com

COLLINS
An Imprint of HarperCollins Publishers

2008
COMMEMORATIVE
STAMP
YEARBOOK

Designed by Journey Group, Inc.

ISBN 978-0-06-166267-6

08 09 10 11 12 ❖/WZ 10 9 8 7 6 5 4 3 2 1

The U.S. Postal Service thanks the Eames Office for its generous contributions to
The 2008 Commemorative Stamp Yearbook.

Yearbook

INTRODUCTION

OUR GRANDPARENTS, Charles and Ray Eames, explored the world through design. They said the role of the designer is essentially that of a good host, anticipating the needs of the guest. With their exquisite visual sense and endless curiosity, process was paramount, and yet their journeys seemed always to bring remarkable things to fruition. This year, the U.S. Postal Service honors the Eameses with stamps that highlight their critical role in architecture, design, film, and the arts.

I don't try to read the minds of my grandparents often, largely because their record is as evocative as it is timeless, but in the case of these stamps, it is easy to make an exception. Charles and Ray would have been extremely grateful, seeing this commemoration for the uniquely privileged moment that it is. This honor is more than some kind of prize; it is truly the spirit of the nation calling attention to what it values. The remarkable lineup of 2008 stamp honorees makes that clear, ranging from scientists and journalists to filmmakers, musicians, and artists. As Charles once said, "Eventually everything connects." They would have particularly enjoyed that these extraordinary connections were happening through stamps.

Charles and Ray wrote to the five of us and our mother, Lucia, quite often. Such letters were magical visual treats ornamenting the day's mail—and you can be sure the stamps were always in an unpretentiously perfect position. It all mattered, because even when you glimpsed the envelope, you were still their guest.

I think they also saw in stamps an echo of what they achieved in furniture, using mass production to create meaningful experiences for people around the globe. When you hold a stamp, whether a first day of issue or not, you hold an original. It is a little piece of beauty reaching the world in its intended form. They loved things like that: what they called "good goods" offering a special connection between maker and recipient. It did not matter whether such things were expensive or not, but only that they had integrity.

This beautifully designed collection of stamps certainly fits the bill and also resonates with their love of imagery. They took hundreds of thousands of photographs which they ultimately donated to the Library of Congress—another deep connection to the American people.

I will close by giving Ray the last word. She used to advise us as kids, "Always be gracious." In her hands, and in yours, stamps are a simple, wonderful way to do just that.

EAMES DEMETRIOS
Director, Eames Office

Charles + Ray EAMES

AS DESIGN PARTNERS as well as husband and wife, Charles and Ray Eames created an extraordinary body of creative work that included furniture, architecture, films, and exhibits reflecting the nation's youthful and inventive outlook after World War II. Without abandoning tradition, they used new materials and technology to create high-quality products that addressed everyday problems and made modern design available to the American public.

Born in St. Louis, Missouri, Charles Eames (1907–1978) was a student of architecture, while California-born Bernice Alexandra "Ray" Kaiser (1912–1988) had studied abstract painting in Manhattan. In 1940, when they met at the Cranbrook Academy of Art in Michigan, they realized that they shared a strong belief in the philosophy that design could improve modern living. They quickly formed an artistic partnership that transcended both architecture and painting. Their work together was distinguished by a fascination with structure, science, and technology, as well as a keen design sensibility and eye for detail.

In 1943, two years after marrying and moving to Los Angeles, they established what would become The Office of Charles and Ray Eames. Located in a large warehouse in Venice, California, the Eames Office was the center of their design ingenuity for more than 40 years.

One of their most popular designs was the molded plywood chair. Introduced in 1946, the chair was mass-produced using a method for bending or molding plywood that the Eameses themselves had developed during the 1940s. The chair was affordable, comfortable, and could be used in virtually any setting—qualities inherent in most pieces of Eames furniture. In the years that followed, Charles and Ray created other attractive and durable pieces; they also pioneered the use of plastic, aluminum, and wire mesh in modern furniture. By 1978, they had put more than 40 designs into production, including sofas, tables, storage units, and airport seating.

EAMES OFFICE

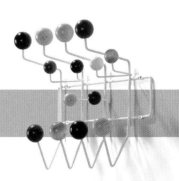

"who ever **said** that ρleasure wasn't . functional?"

— CHARLES EAMES

EAMES HOUSE

"It was the idea of using materials in a different way, materials that could be bought from a catalog," was how Ray Eames described the thinking behind Case Study House #8. When *Arts & Architecture* magazine developed a program to create single-family homes from materials and technologies developed during World War II, the Eameses rose to the challenge. Built quickly with prefabricated parts, this California home consists of two two-story structures made of steel and glass and connected by an open court. Completed in 1949, it was designated a National Historic Landmark in 2006.

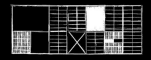

"It makes me feel **guilty** that anybody should have such a **good time** doing what they are **supposed** to do." — CHARLES EAMES

The Eameses also demonstrated that innovations made by wartime industries could be adapted for residential architecture. In 1949, the Eames Office completed its design of Case Study House #8. Located in Pacific Palisades, California, the house was erected quickly using prefabricated parts available at much lower cost than traditional wood. It was part of a program developed by *Arts & Architecture* magazine to create single-family homes from materials and technologies developed during World War II. The award-winning design was praised for its beauty and harmony with the surrounding environment, and it confirmed that modern architecture could be both attractive and affordable.

Interested in images as an effective means of communication, the Eameses made more than 125 slide shows and short films between 1950 and 1978. Their multi-screen presentation *Glimpses of the USA* featured a collage of images of life in the United States during a typical day. Other films, like *Tops* and *Powers of Ten*, imaginatively merged art and science for a popular audience.

According to Charles Eames, he and Ray believed that the role of the designer is essentially that of a good host, anticipating the needs of the guest. Today most of their furniture, and many of their products, are still being made and can be found in private homes and public spaces across the country. More importantly, the Eameses lived as they worked, devoting their days—and nights—to sharing their sense of wonder while encouraging all of us to live creatively.

Opening with this view of a picnicker in a Chicago park, the 1977 Eames film *Powers of Ten* first pulls back to the outer limits of the cosmos, then zooms inward to observe a proton deep within the man's hand. The result is an unforgettable examination of the relative size of objects in the universe.

13]

Latin JAZZ

AN INTEGRAL PART of American music history for more than 100 years, Latin jazz arose alongside jazz in the city of New Orleans, where Caribbean and other cultures melded together during the 19th and early 20th centuries. By the 1930s, this rich blend of American, African, and European influences had spread throughout the United States and Europe.

Freely mixing tradition with experimentation, Latin jazz reached explosive new heights during the 1940s and 1950s when traditional jazz bands adopted the instruments typical of Latin jazz—including conga drums, the bongo, maracas, the cowbell, and other percussion instruments. In turn, Latin jazz adopted some of the characteristics of jazz, such as the use of improvised solos.

As Latin jazz continues to win new fans, the genre has also added several new elements. Although its distinctive rhythm originated in Cuba, musicians who perform Latin jazz have adopted rhythmic patterns from Puerto Rico, the Dominican Republic, Colombia, and Panama. Meanwhile, additional instruments like the piano, saxophone, flute, and trumpet add bright new flavor to the sound of Latin jazz and increase its global appeal.

Featuring a bold graphic design by San Francisco–based artist Michael Bartalos, this stamp depicts three musicians playing bass, piano, and two types of conga drum. "As a fan of both Brazilian and Afro-Cuban Latin jazz," says Bartalos, "it's a thrill to have had the opportunity to design this stamp."

Eager to capture the upbeat, energetic, and romantic spirit that characterizes much of Latin jazz, Bartalos created a tropical evening scene whose colors and shapes convey the multicultural aspects of the music, its percussive and improvisational nature, and its alluring rhythmic complexity—all of which have enriched the musical heritage of the United States.

Cuban-born saxophonist Mario Bauzá, an influential figure in Latin jazz, poses with singer Graciela, circa 1975.

DANCING DAYS

What makes Latin jazz so danceable? The source of that distinctive rhythm is the *clave*, which means "key" or "code" in Spanish. The *clave* pattern stresses unexpected beats in a piece of music while skipping other beats. This syncopation, which originated in Cuba, is practically guaranteed to get you on your feet.

"our idea was to bring **Latin music** up to the standard of the american orchestras."

—MARIO BAUZÁ

American SCIENTISTS

"I DO NOT KNOW what I may appear to the world," Isaac Newton once declared, "but to myself I seem to have been only a boy playing on the sea-shore, and diverting myself in now and then finding a smoother pebble or a prettier shell than ordinary, whilst the great ocean of truth lay all undiscovered before me." With this second American Scientists issuance, the U.S. Postal Service is proud to honor four individuals who, in scrutinizing our universe, labored to fathom Newton's "great ocean of truth" for the benefit of all humanity.

Theoretical physicist John Bardeen (1908–1991) co-invented the transistor, which was arguably the most important invention of the 20th century. Bardeen also collaborated on the first fundamental explanation of superconductivity at low temperatures, a theory which has had a profound impact on many fields of physics.

In collaboration with her husband, biochemist Gerty Cori (1896–1957) made important discoveries—including a new derivative of glucose—that elucidated the steps of carbohydrate metabolism and became the basis for our knowledge of how cells use food and convert it into energy. Their work also contributed to the understanding and treatment of diabetes and other metabolic diseases.

Astronomer Edwin Hubble (1889–1953) played a pivotal role in deciphering the vast and complex nature of the universe. His meticulous studies of spiral nebulae proved the existence of galaxies other than our own Milky Way, paving the way for a revolutionary new understanding that the cosmos contains myriad separate galaxies, or "island universes."

Structural chemist Linus Pauling (1901–1994) determined the nature of the chemical bond linking atoms into molecules. He routinely crossed disciplinary boundaries throughout his career and made significant contributions in several diverse fields. His pioneering work on protein structure was critical in establishing the field of molecular biology, and his studies of hemoglobin led to many findings, including the classification of sickle-cell anemia as a molecular disease.

John Bardeen with a "music box" made possible by his co-invention of the transistor.

Edwin Hubble observed that distant galaxies are receding.

"science is the search for truth"
—linus pauling

Gerty and Carl Cori received a half share of the Nobel Prize for Medicine or Physiology.

Linus Pauling displays his collection of minerals.

17

Minnesota STATEHOOD

MINNESOTA IS a land of water; even the name of the state derives from Dakota Indian words that originally described the color of the Minnesota River. The precise meaning of "Minnesota" has been variously interpreted, from "whitish" or "cloudy water" to the more evocative "sky-blue" or "sky-tinted waters." Thousands of lakes and rivers lie within or along the Minnesota borders, and the state's stunning waterfalls, Mark Twain wryly observed, "do not need a lift from me."

Minnesota became the 32nd state on May 11, 1858. Previously, its 86,939 square miles were part of a large territory that stretched westward from the Wisconsin border to the Missouri River into the future states of North and South Dakota. Today, more than 5 million residents participate in Minnesota's strong, diverse economy, contributing to the production of timber, iron ore, and agricultural crops.

While vital to local industry, the state's spectacular landscapes also prompt Minnesotans to spend their leisure time outdoors, engaging in everything from hiking, camping, and boating to skiing and fishing. Meanwhile, residents and visitors alike take advantage of the state's world-class cultural offerings, including the Minneapolis Institute of Arts, the Minnesota Museum of American Art, the Gammelgarden Museum—and, of course, the U.S. Hockey Hall of Fame.

Commemorating the 150th anniversary of Minnesota statehood, this stamp features a photograph by Richard Hamilton Smith taken at the city of Winona in southeastern Minnesota. In the foreground is a local bridge that spans the main channel of the Mississippi River; the islands above the bridge are part of the Upper Mississippi River National Wildlife and Fish Refuge. Recalling the gorgeous setting that gave Minnesota its name, this vivid image of a beautiful landscape aptly bridges the gap between present and past.

Minnesota Museum
of American Art

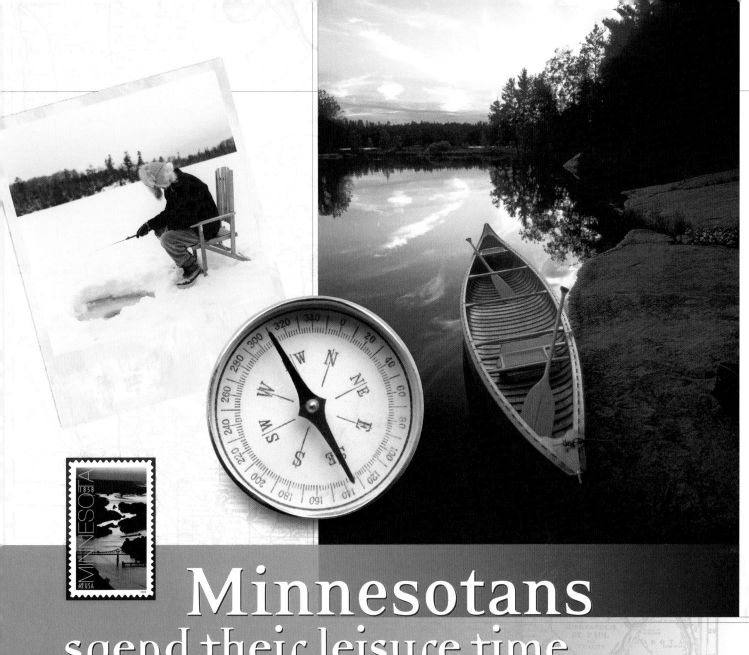

Minnesotans
spend their leisure time
outdoors

Vintage BLACK CINEMA

Duke Ellington,
Black and Tan

THE CORPUS of early African-American cinema belongs to a world lost in time. Even for scholars, researchers, and ardent preservationists, attempting to rediscover that distant era can be a daunting challenge. Countless films have been lost, while others have been mangled. Many have simply been forgotten.

However, in recent years, scholars and celebrities alike have taken a new look at the cinematic treasures that survive. Even as the movies themselves are restored and re-released, vintage film posters have also become collectibles and art objects in their own right. These vivid reminders of a bygone era are eagerly sought by collectors, prominently displayed in museums, and included in traveling exhibitions. The films they advertised are true revelations, all of them shedding new light on the African-American experience as represented in early film.

In the 1921 silent film *The Sport of the Gods,* the family of a wrongfully convicted man flees disgrace in Virginia only to face immorality and temptation in New York City. Based on a novel by Paul Laurence Dunbar, the film was produced by the short-lived Reol Motion Picture Corporation, which made several movies for black audiences.

Remembered as the first screen appearance of Duke Ellington, the 1929 film *Black and Tan* features three songs by Ellington and his Cotton Club Orchestra. In this 19-minute

Louis Jordan,
Caldonia

A Reol
PICTURE

THE SPORT OF THE GODS

by
Paul Laurence Dunbar
AMERICA'S GREATEST RACE POET AND AUTHOR

A TRUE TO LIFE STORY OF
ACTION, THRILLS AND HEART INTEREST
WITH AN ALL-STAR CAST OF COLORED ARTISTS
PRODUCED BY
REOL PRODUCTIONS CORPORATION

Film Title	Black and Tan	The Sport of the Gods	Princess Tam-Tam	Caldonia	Hallelujah
Release Date	1929	1921	1935	1945	1929
Director	Dudley Murphy	Henry J. Vernot	Edmond T. Gréville	William Forest Crouch	King Vidor
Leading Roles	Duke Ellington, Fredi Washington	Leon Williams, Elizabeth Boyer	Josephine Baker	Louis Jordan	Daniel Haynes, Nina Mae McKinney

Nina Mae McKinney,
Hallelujah

Josephine Baker,
Princess Tam-Tam

short, Ellington, playing himself, is in danger of having his piano repossessed. When his fatally ill girlfriend dances at a nightclub, she saves Ellington's music—and asks to hear his "Black and Tan Fantasy" on her deathbed.

One of only four movies to star American-born entertainer Josephine Baker, *Princess Tam-Tam* tells the story of a novelist who discovers a simple African woman, played by Baker, and presents her as a princess to Parisian society. Released in France in 1935, this French-language feature remains a rare film showcase for Baker's singing and dancing.

Released in 1929, *Hallelujah* was one of the first major-studio films to feature an all-black cast. This dramatic story of a field laborer who is seduced away from his community by worldly temptations was filmed primarily in Arkansas and Tennessee. Noted for its portrayal of the rural African-American religious experience, *Hallelujah* earned King Vidor an Oscar nomination for Best Director.

Highlighting the talents of singer, saxophonist, and "jump blues" bandleader Louis Jordan, the 1945 short *Caldonia* is often cited as a precursor of today's music videos. The four musical numbers featured in this 18-minute film also appeared as individual "soundies," short films shown on video jukeboxes at nightclubs and restaurants during the 1940s.

23

LITERARY ARTS:

RAWLINGS

MARJORIE KINNAN RAWLINGS (1896–1953) was born and raised in Washington, DC, but her 1928 move to the Florida scrub country was a blessing for American literature. That year, the aspiring author purchased more than 70 acres of property in the small town of Cross Creek. Inspired by the stories and experiences of her neighbors, she soon began her life's work: documenting the culture of rural Florida with eloquence, honesty, and good humor.

After publishing two novels about life in rural central Florida, Rawlings achieved bestselling success with her third, *The Yearling*. Released in 1938, the book tells the story of Jody Baxter, a 12-year-old boy who adopts a fawn as a pet. The rambunctious fawn soon causes trouble at his family's rural Florida farmstead, forcing Jody's parents to make a difficult decision during uncertain times. The novel garnered rave reviews and earned Rawlings the Pulitzer Prize. *Time* magazine accurately predicted that *The Yearling* stood "a good chance, when adults have finished with it, of finding a permanent place in

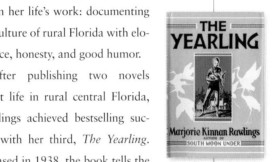

adolescent libraries."

For decades, critics also marveled at Rawlings's nonfiction. When *Cross Creek*, her memoir about her neighbors, was published in 1942, *Time* magazine praised it as a "reminiscent, unhurried, humorous account of how she discovered and took possession of a new United States literary landscape." Readers were so intrigued by the rural culture of Cross Creek that Rawlings gave in to popular demand and published a cookbook that combined exotic recipes with charming local anecdotes.

Today, Rawlings's farmhouse at Cross Creek is the centerpiece of the Marjorie Kinnan Rawlings State Historic Site. The house and farmyard have been designated a National Historic Landmark, and the house is also listed on the National Register of Historic Places. This stamp, the 24th in the Literary Arts series, similarly pays tribute to the places Rawlings loved by evoking the setting of her best-known novel: a long-ago land where a young fawn forever pauses at a Florida watering hole.

"I do not know how anyone can live without some small place of enchantment to turn to."

— *M. K. Rawlings*

FLORIDA FOLKWAYS

Although best known for *The Yearling*, Rawlings also won praise for her memoir *Cross Creek*. Enamored by true tales of the Florida scrub country, the *New York Times* raved that Rawlings "catches the community of land and people ... in the strength and mirth and loveliness of her book."

BLACK HERITAGE:

Chas. W. CHESNUTT

THE MARROW *of* TRADITION

CHARLES W. CHESN[…]

WITH HIS ENGAGING short stories, novels, and essays, Charles W. Chesnutt (1858–1932) addressed a broad range of African-American experiences during the Reconstruction era after the Civil War. Although focused on the problems of the day, he remained optimistic, insisting that "the forces of progress will in the end prevail, and that in time a remedy may be found for every social ill."

Born in Cleveland, Ohio, Chesnutt was the son of a soldier in the Union army who later brought his wife and children to Fayetteville, North Carolina, the city that became the major setting of Chesnutt's fiction. As an adult, Chesnutt returned to Cleveland and studied law, passing the Ohio bar in 1887. He became a wealthy man operating a court stenographic service, but it was his fiction that earned him a place in the American literary pantheon.

Chesnutt's breakthrough came in August 1887 when his short story "The Goophered Grapevine" was published in the *Atlantic Monthly*. One of few stories published by African-American writers at the time, the story was noted for its two narrators: a white northerner who becomes a gentleman farmer and an ex-slave who spins tales of voodoo. The story was collected in the 1899 volume *The Conjure Woman*, which was hailed as "wild indigenous

poetry" by noted critic William Dean Howells. A second collection, *The Wife of His Youth and Other Stories of the Color Line*, followed soon thereafter.

Chesnutt's novels similarly explored the concerns of African Americans. His first published novel, *The House Behind the Cedars*, detailed the frustrated efforts of an accomplished but naive young woman to pass for white. *The Marrow of Tradition*, inspired by a North Carolina race riot, presents a panoramic survey of race relations. A later novel, *In The Colonel's Dream*, argued that the failures of Reconstruction threatened to consign many African Americans to conditions as bad as they had been during the years of slavery.

In 1928, the NAACP awarded Chesnutt the distinguished Spingarn Medal, citing his "pioneer work as a literary artist depicting the life and struggles of Americans of Negro descent." Today Chesnutt is recognized as a major innovator, a singular voice among turn-of-the-century literary realists who probed the color line in American life.

"For one to write about an unfamiliar subject is to court literary disaster. A man writes best about what he knows best."

Chas. W. Chesnutt

"Take Me Out to the BALL GAME"

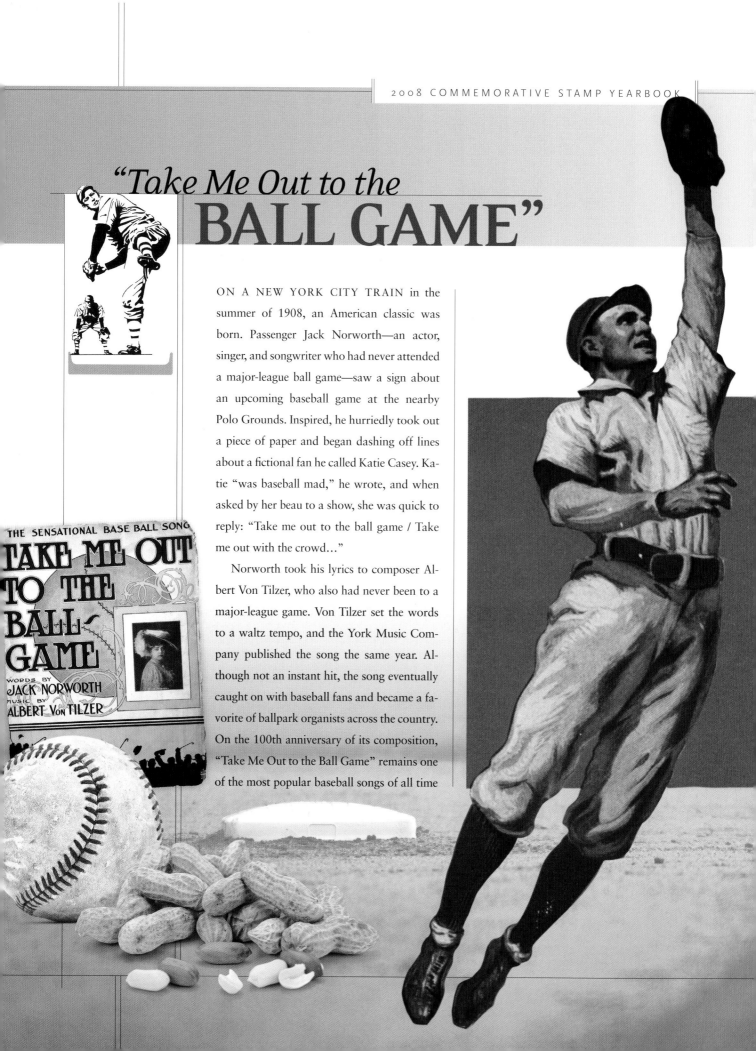

ON A NEW YORK CITY TRAIN in the summer of 1908, an American classic was born. Passenger Jack Norworth—an actor, singer, and songwriter who had never attended a major-league ball game—saw a sign about an upcoming baseball game at the nearby Polo Grounds. Inspired, he hurriedly took out a piece of paper and began dashing off lines about a fictional fan he called Katie Casey. Katie "was baseball mad," he wrote, and when asked by her beau to a show, she was quick to reply: "Take me out to the ball game / Take me out with the crowd…"

Norworth took his lyrics to composer Albert Von Tilzer, who also had never been to a major-league game. Von Tilzer set the words to a waltz tempo, and the York Music Company published the song the same year. Although not an instant hit, the song eventually caught on with baseball fans and became a favorite of ballpark organists across the country. On the 100th anniversary of its composition, "Take Me Out to the Ball Game" remains one of the most popular baseball songs of all time

THE SENSATIONAL BASE BALL SONG

TAKE ME OUT TO THE BALL GAME

WORDS BY JACK NORWORTH
MUSIC BY ALBERT VON TILZER

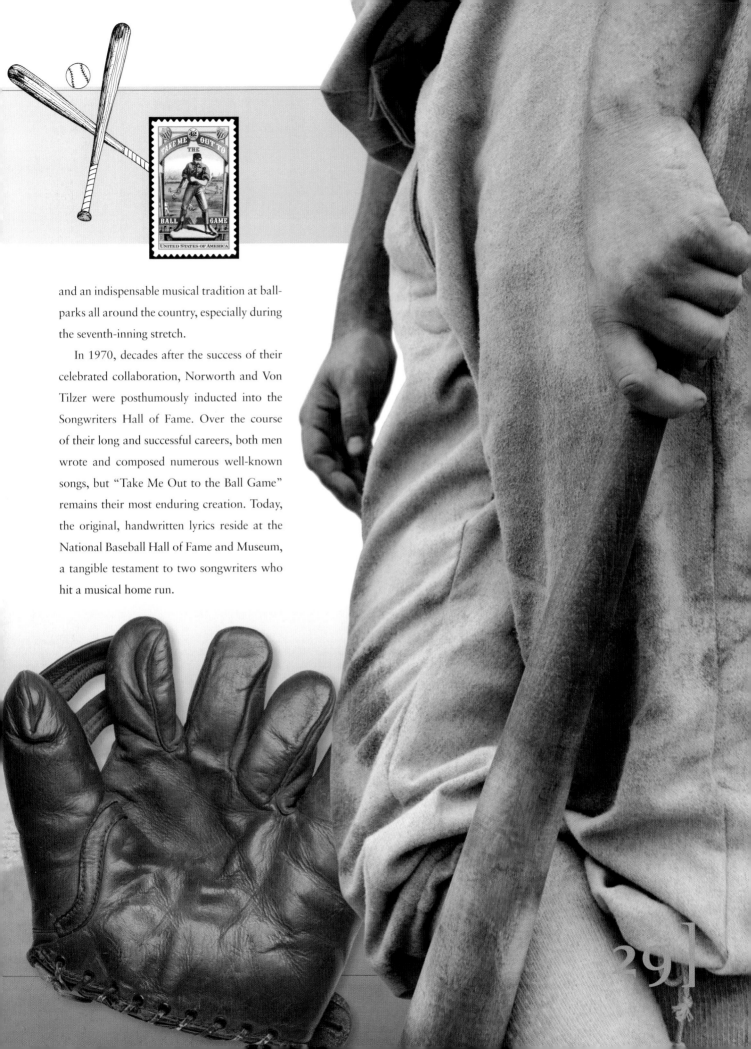

and an indispensable musical tradition at ball-parks all around the country, especially during the seventh-inning stretch.

In 1970, decades after the success of their celebrated collaboration, Norworth and Von Tilzer were posthumously inducted into the Songwriters Hall of Fame. Over the course of their long and successful careers, both men wrote and composed numerous well-known songs, but "Take Me Out to the Ball Game" remains their most enduring creation. Today, the original, handwritten lyrics reside at the National Baseball Hall of Fame and Museum, a tangible testament to two songwriters who hit a musical home run.

Frank

SINATRA

STEREO

Frank Sinatra
September of my years

ARRANGED AND CONDUCTED BY GORDON JENKINS

Featuring such classics as "It Was a Very Good Year" and "September Song," Sinatra's Grammy-winning 1965 album is often considered one of his best.

"i adore making records."

"I ADORE MAKING RECORDS," Frank Sinatra once said. "I'd rather do that than almost anything else." A monumental figure in American popular culture, Sinatra was celebrated as a singer and admired the world over as a supreme interpreter of American popular song.

The son of Italian immigrants, Sinatra was born on December 12, 1915, in Hoboken, New Jersey. As a youth, he sang on street corners with friends. In 1935, he and three others auditioned for a popular radio program; they performed as the "Hoboken Four" and won the talent contest. After touring with them for one season, Sinatra decided to go it alone.

In 1939, Sinatra was singing at a roadhouse in New Jersey when trumpeter and bandleader Harry James hired him to sing with his orchestra. He soon made his first commercial recording, "From the Bottom of My Heart." After several hit songs with trombonist Tommy Dorsey and his band, Sinatra made his breakthrough appearance as a solo performer in New York at the Paramount Theater in December 1942. The hysteria set off by his fans made headlines, and within weeks he had signed recording, movie, and radio contracts.

Sinatra did much to establish and preserve the great American songbook, giving classic songs new life by almost single-handedly inventing the pop album format. During the 1930s, when the boyish crooner evolved into a deeper, more personal interpreter of pop songs, he conveyed the meaning of a lyric with intensity and remarkable nuance. At the same time, he sang with finger-snapping confidence that made him seem the essence of cool. In the years that followed, he worked in almost every conceivable setting, from the great jazz orchestras of Count Basie and Duke Ellington to gentle bossa nova, jukebox pop, and rock-and-roll duets.

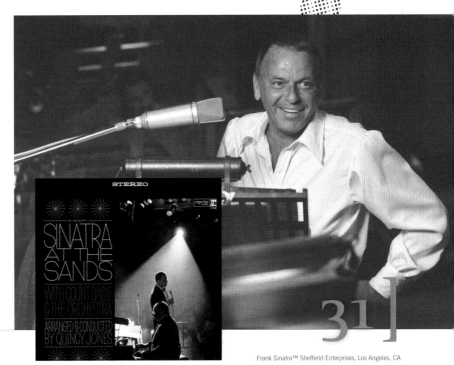

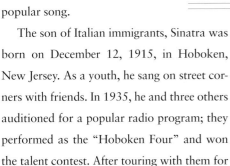

31

Frank Sinatra™ Sheffield Enterprises, Los Angeles, CA

Sinatra directed and appeared as part of the ensemble in the 1965 war movie *None But the Brave*.

Sinatra's talents were also in ample evidence on the silver screen. An Oscar-winning actor who appeared in more than 60 motion pictures, he received a special Academy Award for *The House I Live In*, a short film arguing in favor of racial and religious tolerance. In 1953, his popularity soared to new heights with the release of *From Here to Eternity*. Proving that he was an outstanding dramatic actor, he won an Academy Award for his supporting role as a scrappy Italian-American soldier. Ever versatile, Sinatra performed in several musicals, including *Young at Heart*, *Guys and Dolls*, *High Society*, and *Pal Joey*, but he also excelled in non-singing roles, appearing in the crime caper *Ocean's Eleven* and the political thriller *The Manchurian Candidate*.

In a career studded with accolades, Frank Sinatra won several Grammys, received the Jean Hersholt Humanitarian Award, was recognized at the Kennedy Center Honors, and was awarded the Presidential Medal of Freedom. But "Ol' Blue Eyes" was, at heart, the consummate performer, and the essence of Frank Sinatra is evident in the poignant words he often spoke when bidding farewell to a live audience: "Thank you for letting me sing for you."

In the 1954 film *Young at Heart*, Sinatra plays a grouchy pianist whose outlook on life is brightened by Doris Day.

SINATRA... *best of*

With hundreds of songs in the Sinatra repertoire, every fan can find a favorite—especially from among his most iconic singles.

- Fly Me to the Moon
- I Get a Kick Out of You
- Come Fly With Me
- Luck Be a Lady
- Best is Yet To Come
- All or Nothing At All
- Night and Day
- I've Got You Under My Skin
- Love and Marriage
- All the Way
- Strangers in the Night
- Summer Wind
- That's Life
- My Way

DORIS FRANK
DAY · SINATRA
"**YOUNG AT HEART**"
WITH GIG YOUNG · ETHEL BARRYMORE · DOROTHY MALONE

DIRECTED BY: GORDON DOUGLAS
IN WARNERCOLOR PRINTED IN TECHNICOLOR

Hearts and LOVE: ALL HEART

A LETTER OR CARD can often lift the spirits; this year's new Love stamp suggests that the right correspondence can literally give the heart a lift as well. The design by illustrator Paul Zwolak features a centrally placed bright red heart so full of love that it has lifted its bearer from the ground, perhaps hoping to speed up delivery of its special affection. The stamp's love-struck figure is apparently undaunted by a familiar and oft-used quotation, "A hundred hearts would be too few / To carry all my love for you."

This year, the U.S. Postal Service also reissued the Hearts stamps, which were created especially

for mailing wedding invitations and RSVPs. Featuring vines that form the shape of a heart, they evoke a wide range of intertwined objects, including silver charms and old-fashioned garden gates, and are sure to add an elegant touch to invitations and response cards.

Whether helping to send a love letter through the mail or inviting others to witness a couple professing their love for each other, the universal symbolism embodied by these stamps recalls a truism best expressed by poet Matthew Arnold: "The same heart beats in every human breast."

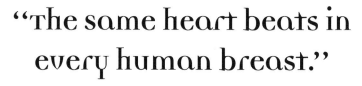

"The same heart beats in every human breast."

— MATTHEW ARNOLD

The Art of Disney:
IMAGINATION

**Pongo and a pup,
101 Dalmatians**

LAUGHTER, CREATIVITY, and dreams are imagination's children. No one knew that better than Walt Disney, the master of imagination who introduced us to new friends and brought us into new worlds.

It all started with a mouse. From the moment Walt Disney first imagined him, Mickey has reminded us that a little laughter goes a long way. Today, it's hard to imagine the world without his familiar smile.

Disney imagination speaks to our romantic side, too. After all, everyone imagines finding true love like Princess Aurora from *Sleeping Beauty*. While we may not have magical helpers like Flora, Fauna, and Merryweather, they remind us that courage, loyalty, and friendship are part of the "happily ever afters" we all dream of.

We also gain new insight into families and friendships from the clear light of Disney imagination. The bond between Pongo and his pups in *101 Dalmatians* shows us our own human ties with tender clarity, while the light-hearted, upbeat relationship between Mowgli and Baloo in *The Jungle Book* proves that friendship and laughter truly are the "bare necessities of life."

From humor to romance, families to friendship, Disney imagination offers more than entertainment. These stamps inspire us to envision richer lives, all because we've felt the power of imagination in making our dreams come true.

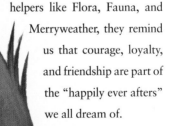

**Baloo and
Mowgli, *The
Jungle Book***

Princess Aurora
with Flora, Fauna,
and Merryweather,
Sleeping Beauty

Mickey Mouse as
Steamboat Willie

37

CELEBRATING LUNAR NEW YEAR:

Year of THE RAT

WHEN THE YEAR OF THE RAT began on February 7, Asian Americans marked the holiday with parades, parties, and other festivities. The U.S. Postal Service commemorated the occasion with this colorful stamp, the first in a visually re-imagined series that acknowl-edges the success of the original Lunar New Year stamps, which were issued from 1992 until 2004, while celebrating the holiday with a highly evocative new look.

Art director Ethel Kessler developed this second series with illustrator Kam Mak, who grew up in Chinatown in New York City. Kessler and Mak chose to focus on realistically painted depictions of common symbols that accompany the annual celebration. This year's festive lanterns, shown in red to indicate good luck, are common decorations at Lunar New Year celebrations, where they are frequently hung in rows.

Although this new Celebrating Lunar New Year series, which continues through 2019, will feature a contemporary look, each design will incorporate elements from the previous series. Collectors will recognize the intricate paper-cut designs by Clarence Lee and the grass-style calligraphy by Lau Bun, both of which graced earlier stamps—a nod to tradition that is sure to surprise and delight.

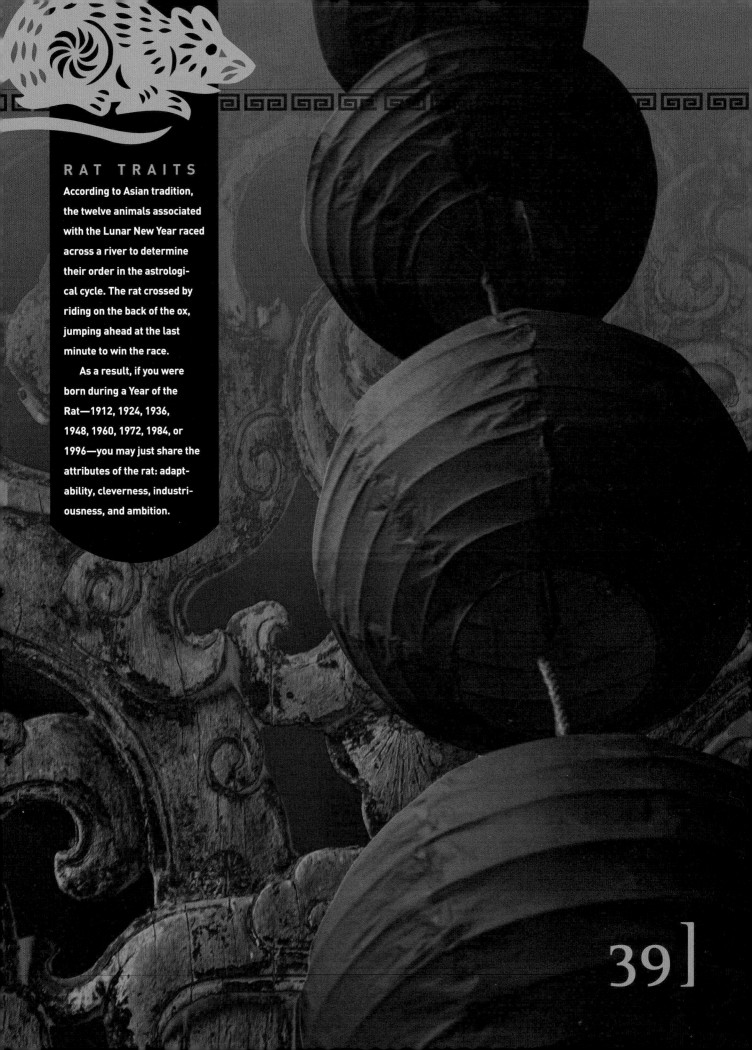

RAT TRAITS

According to Asian tradition, the twelve animals associated with the Lunar New Year raced across a river to determine their order in the astrological cycle. The rat crossed by riding on the back of the ox, jumping ahead at the last minute to win the race.

As a result, if you were born during a Year of the Rat—1912, 1924, 1936, 1948, 1960, 1972, 1984, or 1996—you may just share the attributes of the rat: adaptability, cleverness, industriousness, and ambition.

AMERICA ON THE MOVE:

50s Fins and
CHROME

The design of the 1957 Lincoln Premiere created the illusion of speed.

IN THE YEARS that followed World War II, peace and a booming economy propelled American car design to new heights. Ready to put war and economic depression behind them, an increasingly youthful population demanded larger, faster, and more attractive cars. Americans were eager to spend, and carmakers clamored to satisfy them—and to outdo each other. By the late 1950s, manufacturers had hit on the perfect formula: big, comfortable automobiles with high-powered engines, new safety features, and eye-catching details.

Influenced by contemporary advances in space exploration and jet design, these new cars impressed an adventuresome car-buying public with engines that were more powerful than ever, ranging between 250 and 350 horsepower and capable of accelerating to unprecedented speeds. Yet with standard features like air suspension, power brakes and steering, power windows, and two-way power seats, these vehicles promised not only excitement but also comfort and luxury. Nor did they neglect safety and security: easy handling made driving a breeze, while wraparound windshields increased visibility and power door locks improved security.

Of course, what really set the 1950s car craze in motion were the prominent tail fins and chrome detailing. Understated in 1950, by 1959 tail fins soared nearly four feet off the ground, while the use of chrome had reached extravagant proportions, enveloping the front and rear fenders, wheel rims, window frames, and even the interior trim. Americans went wild for it all—and even though tastes have changed over the years, these cars remain true cultural icons.

Designers work out the details of the 1956 Buick.

By the late 1950s, manufacturers had hit on the perfect formula: big, comfortable automobiles with high-powered engines, new safety features, and eye-catching details.

1959 Cadillac Eldorado
USA 42

1957 Studebaker Golden Hawk
USA 42

1957 Pontiac Safari
USA 42

1957 Lincoln Premiere
USA 42

1957 Chrysler 300C
USA 42

41

AMERICAN TREASURES:

BIERSTADT

Albert Bierstadt, artist

Looking Up the Yosemite Valley, oil on canvas by Albert Bierstadt.

THE GREATEST PAINTERS of the nineteenth century were obsessed with evoking the scale, the scope, and the untrammeled beauty of the American West. Some, like Albert Bierstadt, brilliantly rose to the challenge. Bierstadt was a second-generation member of the Hudson River School, a group of artists devoted to the American landscape. This eighth stamp in the American Treasures series spotlights his magnificent *Valley of the Yosemite*, an 1864 oil-on-paperboard painting that now belongs to the Museum of Fine Arts, Boston.

Born in 1830 near Düsseldorf, Germany, Bierstadt emigrated with his family to the United States two years later and settled in Massachusetts. He received no formal art education prior to 1853, when he returned to Germany to study in the circle of artists active around the Düsseldorf Academy. He then journeyed to Switzerland and Italy in the company of other American painters. Upon his return to the U.S. in 1857, Bierstadt began painting landscapes in New England and upstate New York.

The turning point in Bierstadt's career came in 1859, when he made the first of many trips through the newly opened American frontier. His idealistic western landscapes were immensely popular, especially the grandiose panoramic canvases portraying breathtaking mountain vistas in the Rockies and the Sierra Nevada. In keeping with the Düsseldorf tradition, these huge landscapes were not exact representations of particular locations. Rather, they were finely detailed, highly romanticized views that Bierstadt painted in his studio from the photos and oil sketches he made in the field.

Even at stamp size, *Valley of the Yosemite* demonstrates Bierstadt's effective use of the theatrical, atmospheric lighting and dramatic aerial perspective so characteristic of the Hudson River School. Employing the freshness and immediacy of a field sketch, Bierstadt's painting evokes the sublime grandeur of the unspoiled western wilderness, inviting us to share with the artist a new sense of wonder and awe.

Bridal Veil Falls, Yosemite, another of Bierstadt's masterpieces.

43

LEGENDS OF HOLLYWOOD:

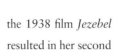

DAVIS

A CONSUMMATE ACTRESS with a magnetic screen presence, Bette Davis (1908–1989) played a wide variety of powerful and complex roles. Famous for her extravagant mannerisms, clipped speech, and zingy one-liners, Davis herself was as spirited and as fiercely independent as many of the characters she portrayed. Never giving an inch in her determination to be the best, she set new precedents for women in the film industry and changed the way Hollywood viewed the contributions of actresses.

Beginning with roles in a few small movies, Davis came into her own with the 1932 film *The Man Who Played God*. Two years later, she gave an electrifying performance as the conniving waitress Mildred Rogers in the highly acclaimed film *Of Human Bondage*. She soared to stardom on the rave reviews, garnering a number of write-in votes for an Academy Award along the way. In 1936, she won the coveted best actress Oscar for her role as Joyce Heath, a former stage star on the skids, in *Dangerous*.

Dissatisfied by the roles she was being offered, Davis took matters into her own hands and left Hollywood. She had planned to make movies in England, but after some legal wrangling she was forced to return and honor her contract. Her studio then offered her a new contract and more appealing roles, a strategy that clearly paid off: her portrayal of headstrong southern belle Julie Marsden in the 1938 film *Jezebel* resulted in her second Academy Award, and she received best actress nominations for five subsequent films.

In 1950, the renowned production *All About Eve* thrust Davis into the limelight again. For her spectacular performance as the brassy, aging Broadway star Margo Channing, she won both the New York Film Critics Circle and the Cannes Film Festival best actress awards and was nominated for a Golden Globe and an Academy Award.

Shortly after accepting a lifetime achievement award at a film festival in Spain, Bette Davis died at the age of 81. She was indomitable to the end: the epitaph on her sarcophagus at Forest Lawn–Hollywood Hills reads, as she had instructed, "She did it the hard way."

According to Hollywood lore, when film magnate Jack
Warner was asked to define the term "movie star,"
he responded with two words: "Bette Davis."

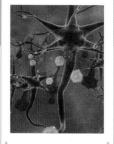

Alzheimer's
AWARENESS

WITH THIS STAMP, the U.S. Postal Service hopes to raise awareness of the issues surrounding Alzheimer's disease, the most common form of dementia among older people. Experts estimate that more than 5 million Americans are living with Alzheimer's disease. There is presently no cure, but scientists around the world are conducting research to learn more about causes and treatment.

Persons suffering from Alzheimer's-related dementia have trouble carrying out daily activities. The disease initially affects the parts of the brain that control language, thought, and memory. Symptoms may include asking the same question repeatedly, becoming lost in familiar places, disorientation during familiar routines, and ignoring personal safety, hygiene, and nutrition. As the disease progresses, perceptual, language, and motor skills deteriorate.

Each case of Alzheimer's disease takes a toll on caregivers as well. There are groups that provide education and support for caregivers and family members. For patients, some drugs have shown promise at ameliorating the symptoms of Alzheimer's during its earlier stages. Following in the footsteps of Alois Alzheimer, the German doctor who first noticed the disease in 1906, modern scientists are studying potential treatments. Envisioning a day when no one else will need to fear, in the words of

Caring for Opa was never easy; often, it was heartbreaking. For more than 50 years, Oma had allowed Opa to run the household, but now Oma had to take command. "It was a task she learned quickly," Strong observed, "but in sadness."

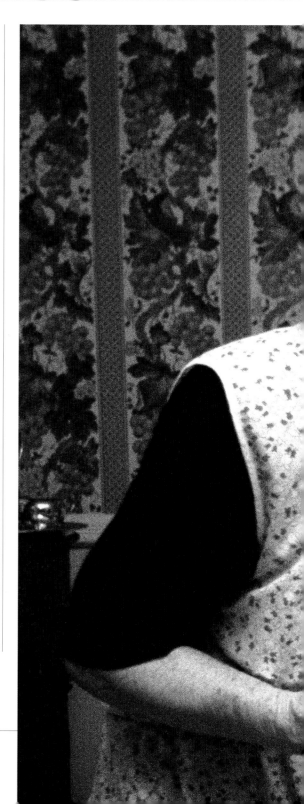

When George Schmid was diagnosed with
Alzheimer's, his wife, Emma, cared for him
and made the disease her daily companion.
Their grandson, photojournalist Bruce Strong,
documented their relationship during this
difficult time. His poignant images of the couple
he knew affectionately as "Oma" and "Opa"
appear on these pages.

Alzheimer's

471

"Remember me when I am gone away,
gone far away into the silent land;
when you can no more hold me by the hand,
Nor I half turn to go, yet turning stay..."

~ CHRISTINA ROSSETTI, "REMEMBER"

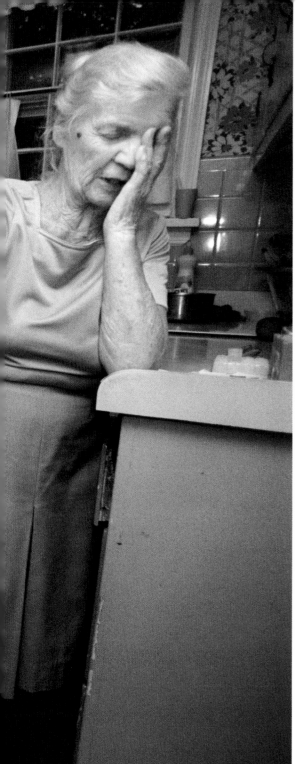

Christina Rossetti, that "the darkness and corruption leave / A vestige of the thoughts that once I had," they continue their research in the hope of eventually preventing or halting the progression of this devastating disease.

As his condition continued to deteriorate, Opa was more likely to awaken confused and combative. Oma grew used to his constant babbling, chattering during meals, complaining about imagined sleights, and recounting stories from his past. But after his death, a strange new silence in her home allowed time for reflection. "I'm so glad I took good care of him," Oma said, "so glad, so glad."

NATURE OF AMERICA:
Great Lakes
DUNES

Spotted sandpiper

ONE OF THE LARGEST freshwater dune systems on Earth flourishes along the shores of the Great Lakes. Some dunes rise close to the water's edge, while others reach far beyond the beaches of sand and stones. The most massive dunes, which lie along the eastern shores of Lake Michigan, are worlds unto themselves, highly dynamic landscapes where wind, water, plants, and animals interact with sand derived from rocky materials dropped by melting glaciers at the end of the last ice age.

On these rugged dunes, life takes root when hardy pioneer vegetation traps and holds sand particles swept ashore by water or wind. Thanks to their tough, fast-growing underground stems, plants such as marram grass and sand reed grass help stabilize dunes by holding those sand grains in place. As a dune stabilizes, more vegetation takes root, and this harsh environment soon becomes amenable to a wide variety of wildlife.

During spring and summer, butterflies and bees gather nectar and pollen from wildflower blossoms. Mayfly nymphs emerge from the gravel and sand of nearby waters and quickly mature into winged adults; they live just long enough to mate and fly back to the water,

The most massive dunes, which lie along the eastern shores of Lake Michigan, are worlds unto themselves.

DUNES FACTS

where females lay their eggs. Other insects busy themselves in the sand. Thread-waisted wasps build ground nests beside clumps of vegetation and feed caterpillars to their developing larvae. Tiger beetles pounce on insect prey, while their larvae wait at the top of vertical burrows and seize passing insects. Antlion larvae excavate conical pitfalls and hide at the bottom, waiting for ants and other potential prey to fall in.

Larger animals thrive here too. Perceptive visitors to the Great Lakes dunes may spot a hognose snake moving slowly through dune grasses, while rustling vegetation may betray the movement of scurrying mammals, including white-footed mice, northern river otters, and curious red foxes.

This tenth issuance in the Nature of America series focuses on Sleeping Bear Dunes National Lakeshore, a federally protected area that encompasses thousands of acres on the northeast shore of Lake Michigan and the nearby islands of North and South Manitou. Here, where tiny seed pods and grains of sand contend with the grand forces of wind and rain, the result is a landscape that teems with new life—a testament to the endless tenacity of nature.

» Most of the sand **that comprises the dunes was derived from rocky materials dropped by melting glaciers at the end of the last ice age.**

» Lakeshore visitors **may glimpse honeycomb-like Petoskey stones, the fossilized remains of a coral species.**

» One plant **whose roots stabilize the dunes is Pitcher's thistle, a rare species found only near the Great Lakes.**

A placid view of Sleeping Bear Dunes National Lakeshore.

51]

GREAT LAKES DUNES

TENTH IN A SERIES

NATURE OF AMERICA

A view of Lake Michigan from Sleeping Bear Dunes National Lakeshore.

The red admiral butterfly

The young red-breasted merganser

The sand cherry

53

Olympic GAMES

AS COMPETITORS FROM around the world streamed into Beijing, China, earlier this year, the U.S. Postal Service continued its tradition of honoring the spirit of athleticism and international unity inspired by the Olympic Games.

The XXIX Olympiad featured approximately 10,500 athletes competing in 302 events in 28 sports, including archery, gymnastics, volleyball, tennis, and tae kwon do. Several new events were added to the Olympic program in 2008: the women's 3,000-meter steeplechase, women's foil and sabre team events, men's and women's 10-kilometer marathon swimming events, and the replacement of the doubles events in table tennis by team events. Men's and women's individual BMX events were also included for the first time.

Although the symbolism of the ancient Olympic Games still influences the modern competition, this year's events were often uniquely and delightfully Chinese. The pictograms that represented each event were reminiscent of ancient inscriptions on bone and bronze objects, the winners' medals were made of gold and jade, and even the torch used in the Olympic torch relay was reminiscent of a paper scroll that displayed auspicious cloud designs.

Featuring a graphic element that resembles the ink mark of a Chinese "chop," a carved wooden stamp used for signatures and seals, this U.S. commemorative offers a similar blend of the ancient and the modern, a reminder that the Olympic Games are steeped in centuries of tradition—but also encourage us to focus on an optimistic future.

The xxix olympiad featured approximately **10,500 athletes** competing in **302 Events.**

55]

American JOURNALISTS

Martha Gellhorn

John Hersey

George Polk

Ruben Salazar

Eric Sevareid

"PUT IT BEFORE them briefly so they will read it, clearly so they will appreciate it, picturesquely so they will remember it and, above all, accurately so they will be guided by its light." Mindful of Joseph Pulitzer's famous credo, these evocative new stamps commemorate five journalists who reported—often at great personal sacrifice—some of the most important stories of the 20th century. Whether working in radio, television, or print, they were drawn to the world's hot spots, ensuring that their reporting might help Americans to respond more intelligently to the world around them.

In a long career that broke new ground for women, Martha Gellhorn (1908–1998) covered many major conflicts, among them the Spanish Civil War, World War II, and the Vietnam War. With its constant focus on harm to civilians, her reporting is often considered a model of moral courage.

A versatile writer, John Hersey (1914–1993) is most famous for *Hiroshima*, which describes what happened when the United States dropped an atomic bomb on the Japanese city. The book has been acclaimed as the greatest work of journalism of the 20th century.

George Polk (1913–1948) filed hard-hitting radio bulletins from Greece describing the strife that erupted there after World War II. He was working on reports of corruption involving U.S. aid when he disappeared; his body was found a week later. The exact circumstances of his death remain a mystery.

Ruben Salazar (1928–1970) was the first Mexican-American journalist to have a major voice in mainstream news media. His writings on the Chicano movement of the 1960s add richly to the historical record. He was shot and killed by a deputy sheriff while covering a protest against the Vietnam War.

Writer and broadcast journalist Eric Sevareid (1912–1992) provided memorable radio coverage of World War II, reporting on the approach of the Germans to Paris, the exodus from the city, and life in London during wartime. His subsequent television commentary on American politics was widely admired.

Named for the intrepid CBS radio reporter, the annual George Polk Awards are among journalism's most prestigious honors.

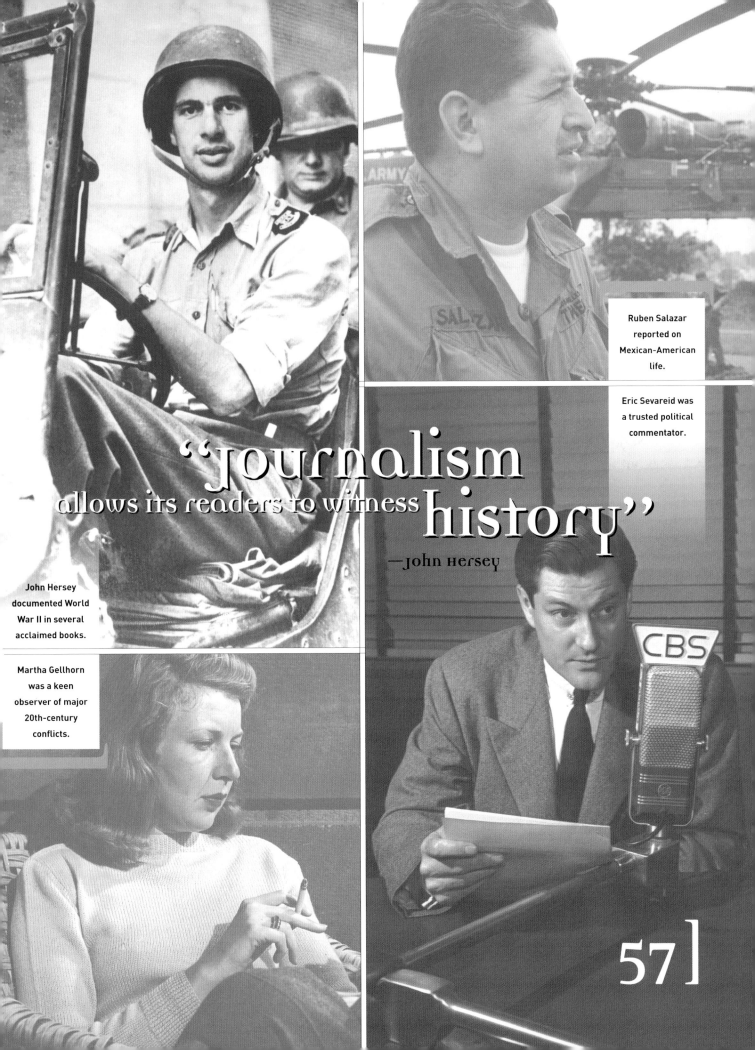

Ruben Salazar reported on Mexican-American life.

Eric Sevareid was a trusted political commentator.

"journalism allows its readers to witness history"

—John Hersey

John Hersey documented World War II in several acclaimed books.

Martha Gellhorn was a keen observer of major 20th-century conflicts.

CBS

Holiday NUTCRACKERS

DURING THE CHRISTMAS SEASON, nutcrackers enhance many time-honored traditions. Appearing in toy stores, under trees, and on mantelpieces, these colorful characters come in all shapes and sizes. Sometimes, they even come alive. One of the most famous nutcrackers, the hero of Tchaikovsky's 1892 ballet suite, dazzles audiences around the world each December as it magically transforms into a prince for an amazed little girl.

This season, four eye-catching nutcracker stamps add colorful, humorous touches to holiday correspondence. With a lantern in one hand and a snowflake-topped staff in the other, a slender, red-suited Santa Claus or "Father Christmas" nutcracker will find his way into millions of mailboxes. He'll be joined by a gold-and-ruby-crowned king, a yellow-jacketed military captain, and a green-garbed drummer with a red drum.

The nutcrackers on these stamps were custom-made by Glenn A. Crider of T.R.C. Designs, Inc., in Mechanicsville, Virginia. Crider based the characters on sketches and notes provided by Sally Andersen-Bruce, who also photographed them. Throughout this Christmas season, these square-jawed creations will delight senders and recipients alike, fostering a fond new set of wistful holiday memories.

NUTCRACKER BALLET

Composed by Pyotr Ilich Tchaikovsky during the early 1890s, *The Nutcracker* is one of the most popular ballets of all time, especially during Christmas. With its battle between the Nutcracker Prince and the Mouse King, as well as its visions of the Land of the Sugar Plum Fairies, Tchaikovsky's masterpiece inspires new generations to imagine the swashbuckling thoughts behind those mysterious smiles.

59

CHRISTMAS:

Virgin and Child with the Young John the Baptist by

SANDRO BOTTICELLI

**Sandro Botticelli,
Renaissance painter**

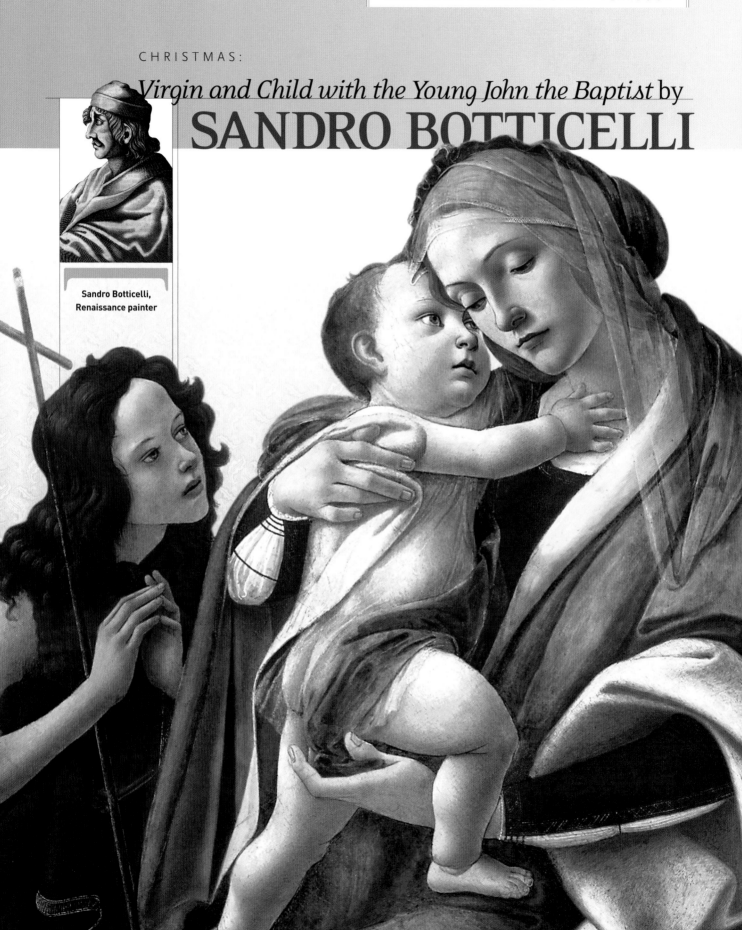

Sandro Botticelli was an important figure in the early Italian Renaissance; two of his works, *The Birth of Venus* and *Primavera* (or *The Allegory of Spring*), have become especially iconic to modern eyes. After his death, Botticelli's role in the Florentine school of painting inspired Giorgio Vasari, who composed famous biographies of Renaissance artists, to praise Botticelli's rise to prominence and to suggest that he had helped make the mid-15th century "a golden age for men of intellect."

ONE OF THE GREATEST painters of the Florentine Renaissance, Sandro Botticelli (circa 1445–1510) excelled at portraiture, depictions of mythological subjects, and Christian devotional painting. As a youth, he was apprenticed first to a goldsmith and then to Fra Filippo Lippi, a master painter. His talent quickly gained him recognition, winning him the patronage of the powerful Medici family. During the early 1480s, he also assisted in the first phase of the decoration of the Sistine Chapel. Later, as a recognized master, he ran a large and active workshop and trained many artists, including Filippino Lippi, the son of the painter who had earlier trained him.

This year's Christmas stamp features Botticelli's *Virgin and Child with the Young John the Baptist* (detail shown at left), which dates from around 1490 and is now in the collection of the Cleveland Museum of Art. This painting—tempera and oil on wood—presents one of the most common figural groups in Christian art. Its beautifully rendered scene captures the tender relationship between mother and child and suggests Mary's foreknowledge of Christ's fate. The facial expression of John the Baptist, seen standing to the side in a prayerful pose, also hints at a heightened awareness.

According to art historians, assistants probably painted parts of this great work; the Virgin's face, the best preserved section of the painting, was most likely painted by Botticelli himself. Her robes, particularly her left arm and the yellow lining of the sleeve, have been restored. More than five centuries later, we owe a debt of gratitude to the assistants and scholars alike who helped to preserve this masterpiece; they have provided us with another depiction of a cherished Christmas theme.

COVER
© U.S. Postal Service, art by Katie Doka

TITLE PAGE
© Thomas Dix, Germany, Courtesy Vitra Design Museum

CHARLES + RAY EAMES
Page 10: Wire Mesh chair, Eames Office logo and Molded Plywood Chair © Eames Office LLC. Courtesy Library of Congress, Prints and Photographs Division, The Work of Charles and Ray Eames; Eames Storage Unit and Hang-It-All © Thomas Dix, Germany, Courtesy Vitra Design Museum
Page 11: Lounge Chair and Ottoman © Thomas Dix, Germany, Courtesy Vitra Design Museum; Case Study House #8 © Tim Street-Porter; Charles and Ray Eames at Case Study House #8 © Eames Office LLC. Courtesy Library of Congress, Prints and Photographs Division, The Works of Charles and Ray Eames
Page 12: (top) Photograph by Andrew Neuhart © Eames Office LLC. Courtesy Library of Congress, Prints and Photographs Division, The Work of Charles and Ray Eames; (center left) © Eames Office LLC. Courtesy Library of Congress, Prints and Photographs Division, The Work of Charles and Ray Eames; (bottom left) © Thomas Dix, Germany, Courtesy Vitra Design Museum; (second from left) © U.S. Postal Service, photography by Sally Andersen-Bruce; (third from left) © Eames Office LLC. Courtesy Library of Congress, Prints and Photographs Division, The Work of Charles and Ray Eames; (fourth from left) Charles Eames, LCM Low Side Chair. 1946. Molded walnut-veneered plywood, chromium steel rods and rubber shock mounts, 27 3/8" X 22 1/4" X 25 3/8". Gift of the manufacturer. Accession Number 156.1973. Digital Image © The Museum of Modern Art/Licensed by Scala/Art Resource, NY; film still from *Powers of Ten* © Eames Office LLC. Courtesy Library of Congress, Prints and Photographs Division, The Work of Charles and Ray Eames

LATIN JAZZ
Page 14: (top left) © U.S. Postal Service, art by Michael Bartalos; (bottom, right) Frank Driggs Collection/Getty Images
Page 15: (top left) © numb/Alamy; (top right) Time & Life Pictures/Getty Images; (bottom) © U.S. Postal Service, art by Michael Bartalos

AMERICAN SCIENTISTS
Page 16: (top left) clipart.com; (bottom left) Courtesy NASA/Johns Hopkins University Applied Physics Laboratory/Carnegie Institution of Washington, Image Control Number PIA10179; (Hubble stamp image) Edwin Hubble, Edwin Hubble Collection, Huntington Library
Page 17: (clockwise from top left) Courtesy William A. Bardeen, Bardeen Family Archives; Courtesy Washington University School of Medicine; Time & Life Pictures/Getty Images; © Bettmann/Corbis

MINNESOTA STATEHOOD
Page 18: (background) iStockphoto; (top left) Visions of America/Joe Sohm/Digital Vision/Getty Images; (bottom left) Paul Chesley/Stone/Getty Images; (gold frame) Anastasiya Maksymenko/iStockphoto
Page 19: (background) iStockphoto; (clockwise from top left) Lenora Gim/Photonica/Getty Images; © 2008 Gerald Brimacombe; © 2008 Gerald Brimacombe; Joel Sartore/National Geographic/Getty Images; Christine Balderas/iStockphoto

VINTAGE BLACK CINEMA
Page 20: (top left) Michael Ochs Archives/Getty Images; (bottom left) James Warren/iStockphoto; (bottom right) Michael Ochs Archives/Getty Images
Page 21: AllPosters.com
Page 22: Courtesy University of California, Los Angeles, Department of Special Collections, Chester E. Young Research Library
Page 23: (left) Michael Ochs Archives/Getty Images; (top right) © John Springer Collection/Corbis

LITERARY ARTS: MARJORIE KINNAN RAWLINGS
Page 24: (top left) clipart.com; (center left) Roel Smart/iStockphoto; (center) Rare Books and Special Collections, Thomas Cooper Library, The University of South Carolina
Page 25: (top left) Rare Books and Special Collections, Thomas Cooper Library, The University of South Carolina; (top) Courtesy of Marjorie Kinnan Rawlings Manuscript Collection, Department of Special and Area Studies Collections, George A. Smathers Libraries, University of Florida; photograph by *Sunday Magazine.*

BLACK HERITAGE: CHARLES W. CHESNUTT
Page 26: (top left) clipart.com; (full page) Courtesy Cleveland Public Library Special Collections
Pages 26–27: (books) Courtesy Cleveland Public Library Special Collections
Page 27: (background) iStockphoto

"TAKE ME OUT TO THE BALL GAME"
Page 28: (top left) clipart.com; (center left) Diamond Images/Getty Images; (bottom left, both) iStockphoto; (right) The Palma Collection/Photodisc/Getty Images
Pages 28–29: Fred Hall/iStockphoto
Page 29: (top left) clipart.com; (bottom left) Christine Balderas/iStockphoto; (right) Jared Leeds/Aurora/Getty Images

FRANK SINATRA
Page 30: (top left) clipart.com; (bottom) © 1978 Sid Avery/MPTV.net; (center right) Provided courtesy of Reprise Records, a Warner Music Group Company. Album cover image provided by MPTV.net.

Page 31: (right) clipart.com; (bottom right) © 1978 Ed Thrasher/MPTV.net; (inset) Provided courtesy of Reprise Records, a Warner Music Group Company. Album cover image provided by MPTV.net. Album cover photo of Frank Sinatra performing by John Bryson.

Page 32: (top) NONE BUT THE BRAVE (1965) © Somerset Trust. Licensed by: Warner Bros. Entertainment Inc. All Rights Reserved. Photo courtesy MPTV.net; (bottom) © 1978 Sid Avery/MPTV.net

Page 33: Courtesy Photofest

HEARTS and LOVE: ALL HEART
Page 34: (top) clipart.com; (bottom) Maria Taglienti-Molinari/Jupiterimages

Pages 34–35: (background and border pattern) Peter Zelei/iStockphoto

Page 35: (clockwise from top left) © Charles Gullung/zefa/Corbis; Digital Vision/Getty Images; © Simon Jarratt/Corbis; Photo courtesy Ron Londen; Mikhail Bistrov/iStockphoto

THE ART OF DISNEY: IMAGINATION
Pages 36–37: Disney Materials © Disney

CELEBRATING LUNAR NEW YEAR: YEAR OF THE RAT
Page 38: (top) Khoo Eng Yow/iStockphoto; (center four photos) © Tamara Reynolds Photography/Represented by RepGirl, Inc; (center bottom) © Ken Seet/Corbis; (left bottom) © U.S. Postal Service, calligraphy by Spencer Yuen

Page 39: Hsing-Wen Hsu/iStockphoto; (left top) © U.S. Postal Service, art by Clarence Lee

AMERICA ON THE MOVE: 50s FINS AND CHROME
Page 40: (top and bottom left) © U.S. Postal Service, art by Art M. Fitzpatrick; (center right) © 2008 GM Corp. Used with permission, GM Media Archive

Page 41: © Bruce Benedict/Transtock/Corbis

AMERICAN TREASURES: ALBERT BIERSTADT
Page 42: (top left) © Corbis; (bottom left) Courtesy The Haggin Museum, Haggin Collection, Stockton, California; (right) © Hedda Gjerpen/iStockphoto; Albert Bierstadt, *Valley of the Yosemite*, 1864, Museum of Fine Arts, Boston, Gift of Martha C. Karolik for the M. and M. Karolik Collection of American Paintings, 1815–1865. Photograph © 2007 Museum of Fine Arts, Boston.

Page 43: © North Carolina Museum of Art/Corbis

LEGENDS OF HOLLYWOOD: BETTE DAVIS
Page 44: (top left) iStockphoto; (second from top) Alfred Eisenstaedt/Time & Life Pictures/Getty Images; (third from top) THE LETTER (1940) © Turner Entertainment Co. A Warner Bros. Entertainment Company. All Rights Reserved, photo courtesy Photofest; (bottom left) Alfred Eisenstaedt/Time & Life Pictures/Getty Images; (bottom right) JEZEBEL (1938) © Turner Entertainment Co. A Warner Bros. Entertainment Company. All Rights Reserved, photo courtesy Photofest

Page 45: JEZEBEL (1938) © Turner Entertainment Co. A Warner Bros. Entertainment Company. All Rights Reserved, artwork courtesy Photofest

ALZHEIMER'S AWARENESS
Page 46: (top left) Courtesy TPT/Twin Cities Pubic Television; (bottom left) Edyta Linek/iStockphoto

Pages 46–47: © Bruce Strong/LightChasers.com

Pages 48–49: © Bruce Strong/LightChasers.com

NATURE OF AMERICA: GREAT LAKES DUNES
Page 50: (top) Paul Tessier/iStockphoto

Pages 50–51: © Corbis

Page 51: (top right) © Andrew Parkinson/Corbis

Pages 52–53: © William Manning/Corbis

Page 53: (clockwise from top) © William Manning/Corbis; Hannu Hautala/Nordic Pictures/Getty Images; © Kerry Kelly, Friends of Sleeping Bear Dunes, Inc.; Felix Labhardt/Taxi/Getty Images

OLYMPIC GAMES
Page 54: (background) © U.S. Postal Service, art by Katie Doka; (top) China Photos/Getty Images; (bottom) Donald Miralle/Getty Images

Page 55: (clockwise from top left) Joe Patronite/Getty Images; Photo and Co/Getty Images; CO Rentmeester/Getty Images; Shaun Botterill/Getty Images

AMERICAN JOURNALISTS
Page 56: (top) clipart.com; (bottom right) CBS/Landov; (Salazar stamp image) Ruben Salazar, from the *Los Angeles Times* Photographic Archive (Collection 1429), Department of Special Collections, Charles E. Young Research Library, UCLA

Page 57: (clockwise from top left) © Bettmann/Corbis; Courtesy of Lisa Salazar Johnson; CBS/Landov; Lloyd Arnold/JFK Library and Museum

HOLIDAY NUTCRACKERS
Page 58: (top) Peter Baxter/iStockphoto; (bottom center) © U.S. Postal Service, nutcracker created by Glenn A. Crider, photography by Sally Andersen-Bruce

Page 59: (clockwise from top) Kati Molin/iStockphoto; Stockbyte/Getty Images; Victor Burnside/iStockphoto

CHRISTMAS: VIRGIN AND CHILD WITH THE YOUNG JOHN THE BAPTIST BY SANDRO BOTICELLI
Pages 60–61: (background) iStockphoto

Page 60: (top) Hulton Archive/Getty Images; (bottom) Sandro Botticelli (Italian, 1444/5-1510) and workshop. *Virgin and Child with the Young John the Baptist*, c. 1490. Tempera and oil on wood; D: 68 cm. © The Cleveland Museum of Art, Leonard C. Hanna, Jr. Fund 1970.160

Page 61: (top) *Madonna and Child* (oil on panel), Botticelli, Sandro (1444/5-1510) (studio of)/Fitzwilliam Museum, University of Cambridge, UK/The Bridgeman Art Library; (round frame around painting) iStockphoto; (bottom) clipart.com

These stamps and this stamp-collecting book were produced by Stamp Services, Government Relations, United States Postal Service.

JOHN E. POTTER
Postmaster General, Chief Executive Officer

MARIE THERESE DOMINGUEZ
Vice President, Government Relations and Public Policy

DAVID E. FAILOR
Executive Director, Stamp Services

Special thanks are extended to the following individuals for their contributions to the production of this book:

UNITED STATES POSTAL SERVICE

TERRENCE W. McCAFFREY
Manager, Stamp Development

CINDY L. TACKETT
Manager, Stamp Products and Exhibitions

SONJA D. EDISON
Project Manager

THE CITIZENS' STAMP ADVISORY COMMITTEE

BENJAMIN F. BAILAR
CARY R. BRICK
MICHAEL R. BROCK
DONNA DE VARONA
JEAN PICKER FIRSTENBERG
DR. HENRY LOUIS GATES, JR.
SYLVIA HARRIS
JESSICA HELFAND
I. MICHAEL HEYMAN
JOHN M. HOTCHNER
KARL MALDEN
JOAN A. MONDALE
B. MARTIN PEDERSEN
RONALD A. ROBINSON
CLARA RODRIGUEZ

HARPERCOLLINS PUBLISHERS

STEPHANIE MEYERS
Associate Editor, Collins

LUCY ALBANESE
Design Director, General Books Group

SUSAN KOSKO
Production Director, General Books Group

TOM McNELLIS
Senior Production Editor

JOURNEY GROUP, INC.

MICHAEL RYAN
Design Director

ZACHARY BRYANT
KRISTEN KIMMEL
MATTHEW PAMER
LISA RYAN
HOPE VOELKEL
Design & Creative Assistance

GREGORY BREEDING
Creative Director

JENNIFER ARNOLD
Account Director

PHOTOASSIST, INC.

MARY STEPHANOS
JEFF SYPECK
Editorial Consultants

MICHAEL OWENS
Images Coordinator

JESSICA GREEN
KATE GRIFFIN
NANCY OSTERTAG
MICHAEL OWENS
CRISTEN WILLS
Images Research

SARAH HANDWERGER
MICHAEL OWENS
Rights and Permissions

JESSICA GREEN
CRISTEN WILLS
Traffic Coordinators